THE CATHOLIC UNIVERSITY
AND THE FAITH

The Aquinas Lecture, 1978

THE CATHOLIC UNIVERSITY AND THE FAITH

Under the auspices of the
Wisconsin-Alpha Chapter of Phi Sigma Tau

By
FRANCIS C. WADE, S.J.

MARQUETTE UNIVERSITY PRESS
MILWAUKEE
1978

LC 487
W 24X

In lumine tuo videbimus lumen
(Ps. 35:10).

Prefatory

The Wisconsin Alpha Chapter of Phi Sigma Tau, the National Honor Society for Philosophy at Marquette University, each year invites a scholar to deliver a lecture in honor of St. Thomas Aquinas. This year the lecture was delivered on Sunday, March 5, 1978.

The 1978 Aquinas Lecture *The Catholic University and the Faith* was delivered in Todd Wehr Chemistry by the Reverend Francis C. Wade, S.J., Professor of Philosophy at Marquette University.

Fr. Wade was born on November 11, 1907 at Whitesboro, Texas. He entered the Society of Jesus on September 1, 1925 at Florissant, Missouri. He earned an A.B. in 1930 at Xavier University, Cincinnati, and an M.A. in 1932 and an S.T.L. in 1939 at Saint Louis University. After five years of teaching philosophy at Rockhurst College in Kansas City, Fr. Wade came to Marquette University in 1945 and has taught philosophy at Marquette for thirty-three years. In 1954 he became associate professor and in 1965 professor. His excellence as a teacher has been consistently acknowledged by his students and was formally recognized by the University's Award for Teaching Excellence in 1970.

Though Fr. Wade's publications in philosophy range over the areas of logic, metaphysics, ethics and mediaeval philosophy, his philosophical concern with the role of teaching in a Catholic university has been a recurrent theme in his articles and reviews. In 1963 his book, *Teaching and Morality,* appeared. He has translated *John of St. Thomas, Outlines of Formal Logic* and is co-translator of *Cajetan's Commentary on Being and Essence of St. Thomas Aquinas.* Among his more recent writings are: "On Violence," *The Journal of Philosphy,* 1971; "In Defense of Socrates," *The Review of Metaphysics,* 1971; " 'To Force' and 'To Do Violence To'," *The Journal of Value Inquiry,* 1975; and "Potentiality in the Abortion Discussion," *The Review of Metaphysics,* 1975.

To these publications Phi Sigma Tau is pleased to add: *The Catholic University and the Faith.*

The Catholic University and the Faith

A university can be described today as a community of scholars, actual and potential, dedicated to preserving and extending knowledge. The two actions generally considered as most proper to the university are teaching and research. How these two activities are interrelated will depend on the history and the ideals of each university. Using this pattern, we can say that a Catholic university is a community of scholars, actual and potential, who wish to carry on teaching and research within the context of their Catholic faith. How the activities of teaching and research are interrelated will again depend on the history and ideals of each Catholic university.

My focusing on teaching and research is not intended to deny that there are other important activities in a university. Especially does this need to be said about a contemporary Catholic university, which takes seriously its duty to foster community. Yet it is still true today as in the past that the bone structure of any university is constituted by its teaching and research, no matter how these bones may be variously fleshed out and diligently clothed in the contemporary academic or even religious fashions. My interest is to look to the bone structure of the Catholic University, as that which will sustain and unify whatever flesh or clothing seems necessary at any one time. I may as well say here in the beginning that much, though not all, of what I say about the Catholic university can also be said about any Christian university that takes the Christian faith as a serious part of the intellectual life.

The role of the Catholic university can be stated by looking to the needs that it seeks to fulfill. First, it meets a need of the Catholic community. The Church has the mission of salvation to all classes of people. In order to present its truth to the highly educated, a group that is becoming increasingly large in America today, the Church must express its teachings and values in a fully developed and intellectually precise form. Hence the need for an institution dedicated to such pursuit. At the same time, and to just as great an extent, the Church needs to grow in its own understanding of the revelation it has received. Every advance in human knowledge can be of aid in understanding this revelation. Hence the need of the Church for a university as an human endeavor to keep its understanding of revelation strong and living.[1] Notice, too, that this need is not for a religious institution; the need is for an academic institution.[2]

Its specific character of being academic points to the second need that the Catholic university seeks to fulfill. As an institution in a pluralist society it serves to present, explicate and explore the insights that are generally Christian, as well as those that are specifically Catholic. Pluralism, as public policy, welcomes many explanatory and value systems and encourages the advocates of each to add to the common discussion and common decisions. Indeed, the vigor of a pluralist society demands that the proponents of the manifold value systems identify themselves and give a clear and vigorous articulation of what they stand for. The Catholic university serves this role in the world of Academe, the world of preserving and extending knowledge. Its task is to contribute its insights and discoveries to the ongoing academic project and in turn be modified by the insights and discoveries of Academe. If there were no Catholic universities, the academic world would be the poorer for it.

II

The reason Academe would be poorer is that it would lack an advocate of mystery. My saying that the Catholic university advocates mystery may sound strange to some and totally unacceptable to others. Let me explain what I mean by mystery.

In common usage, mystery may mean simply what we do not know. A man, for example, may say that it is a mystery to him why his car will not start. This is a valid usage because the root meaning of mystery is the hidden or secret. This was the original usage of mystery in Western thought, where it was applied to the secret rites and ceremonies of ancient pagan religions, such as the Eleusinian mysteries. These actions and prayers were hidden from all except those initiated into the religion. A more contemporary usage is that of Gabriel Marcel, who distinguished a problem from a mystery. Problems are presented when the data is fully objective so that I can lay siege to the problem and solve it. A mystery, by comparison, is something I myself am involved in and I cannot accurately distinguish between what is in me and what is before me.[3] An example is the question: What am I? Another contemporary, Milton K. Munitz, applies mystery to a question which is legitimate but for which we have not and in principle cannot find an answer, such as the question: Why is there a world at all?[4] A third contemporary usage is that employed by Catholic theologians. They distinguish between supernatural and natural mysteries. Natural mysteries are naturally known truths that remain obscure because the reality contains more than our concepts can explicate fully. Examples of these are animal instinct, sense experience, free will. Supernatural mysteries are truths that cannot be known without revelation of God and even after such revelation remain obscure to us because of the sublimity of their objects. Some examples are: the communication of divine life within the Trinity, the communication of divine life to a created nature in the Incarnation, the elevation of a created nature to share in the divine life by grace or glory.[5]

I have listed these uses of mystery without dwelling on their similarities and differences. For my purposes, they all have one common characteristic: they all apply mystery to a limited sort of data or question or reality and employ their meaning in order to distinguish the mysterious from the non-mysterious. I should like to take a different tack so as to catch another wind in my sails. Go back to the root meaning of mystery as the secret and hidden. Then apply the term to things insofar as they have layers of further deeper and hidden meaning. By mystery, then, I mean that things, all things, in their own right present inexhaustible possibilities for more human knowledge. And to say that one recognizes mystery is not to divide things into the mysterious and the non-mysterious. It is rather to point to an aspect of all existents, their continuing fecundity for human knowledge.

This insight is founded squarely in the Christian view of the world. What is is made by God, either directly by His creative act or indirectly through beings He has made to be causes of other things. Yet all of them share in expressing some excellence of their ultimate cause. The one excellence of God they all share in most radically is that they, like God and because of God, exist. And since the existence of God is the center and core of His own mysteriousness, every existent by participating in existence also participates in the mysteriousness of God. God as infinite being is an inexhaustible object for knowledge; the existents of this world are also inexhaustible objects for knowledge to the extent that they participate in God's existence. Add to this existential participation the role all things play in being the beneficiaries of the redeeming life of Christ, and you see why the Christian has respect for all that is. Respect for God translates into respect for the things God has made and redeemed. The theological way to state this position is to say that a Christian should find God in all things.

Now let a Christian begin to philosophize. From his faith he knows that all things are mysterious and therefore are inexhaustible sources of knowledge. His proper philosophical stance, then, is to be open to all reality. But not just any kind of openness will do. Neutrality, for example, is a kind of openness. It consists in being open to either of two sides or answers to a question in the sense that neither is accepted. On occasion neutrality may be called for but can hardly be considered a Christian ideal. A second meaning of openness is a formal one; that is, one is simply open or prepared to consider any and all facts. No doubt, formal openness is better than prejudice; still openness for its own sake is basically incomplete because it leads nowhere. There must be third meaning of openness. To get a leg up on this third meaning, recall that the human mind wants to know because it is made to do just this. Its finality is to know and this requires commitment[6] to the truth. This means that man's mind is open in order to learn, i.e. to close on the truth, and this is no longer neutrality or formal openness, but the state of being committed to the truth of what is. Thus the third meaning, the one I am proposing as proper for a Christian, includes two elements: 1) readiness before reality as it is; and 2) acceptance of reality as it is. Both factors can be caught up in the phrase, "openness to all that is." All that is, being, is what the mind is open to and all that is, being, is what the mind closes on. At the same time, openness to all that is is self-corrective: what is can demand a change in a former commitment that was inadequately founded on reality. The Christian, because open to all that is, is also committed to what is.

III

At this point we need to consider the role that "what is" or fact plays in knowledge. In this consideration we shall use speculative rather than practical knowledge. Aristotle distinguishes two major kinds of knowledge: 1) speculative or reporting knowledge that deals with what is; and 2) practical knowledge that deals with how to do or make.[7] The two knowledges differ in their starting points. Thomistic metaphysicians tell us that being as true is the first principle or starting point of speculative knowledge. What they mean is that there must be something before we can say that it is or what it is. They also tell us that the first principle of practical knowledge is being as good, but they add that the second principle is being as true.[8] What they mean is that no one makes shoes unless he thinks it is worthwhile (good) to do so, and it is not good shoemaking if what is made are not shoes.

Since even in practical knowledge being (what is) is finally determinative, I shall confine my analysis to speculative knowledge.

Speculative knowledge, we said, deals with facts. This could mean no more than saying that facts are simply the condition of knowing, much as the curtains being open is a condition of sunlight in the room. Facts are much more than conditions. We said above that facts are the first principle of knowledge. This is to say that facts *cause* knowledge and nothing else will. In one sense you cause your own knowing. In another sense the facts cause your knowing. No matter how hard you try, you cannot know unless there is an object known. The reason is that knowledge, though it resides in the knower, is always about the known. What is peculiar to knowledge is that while it specifies or qualifies the knower—the knowledge is yours—it does its specifying or qualifying in terms of the known. Thus the knowledge called biology is the specification of the biologist in terms of the facts about the living. Without these facts or what is taken for biological facts there could be no knowledge of biology. And this is true of all knowledge. Given a being, it can act on human knowing powers to specify them. The mind, specified by the thing, is a knowing mind. Where there is no thing to do the specifying, there is no specification, that is, no knowledge. What this comes down to is that facts talk to our minds and nothing else does. Even when men talk to us, it is the facts that talk through them. That is the reason why we understand nothing when a man speaks a language unknown to us. The sounds he makes we know; what we do not know are the things his sounds refer to and without such things we do not know what he is saying.

Let me stop a moment to explain what I mean by a fact. Contemporary discussions emphasize incompatible meanings of fact. J. L. Austin contends that fact applies most properly to "something in the world."[9] P. F. Strawson denies this and argues that fact applies primarily to statements, in the usage: 'The fact that so-and-so.'[10] In this discussion Austin seems to have the better case when he points out that according to the Oxford English Dictionary (1933), the usage of 'the fact that' is given ". . . as a comparative recent linguistic device for avoiding gerundial constructions as subjects of sentences or as domains of prepositions: i.e. in order not to say . . . 'the kitchen's being drafty annoyed him' . . . we say 'the fact that the kitchen was drafty annoyed him. . . .'"[11] It is hard to agree with Strawson that such a late substitutional usage can be the preferred use of a word that had pretty well set its meaning in the eighteenth century, where fact meant, according to the Oxford Dictionary: "something that has really occurred or is actually the case; something certainly known to be of this character; hence, a particular truth known by actual observation or authentic testimony, as opposed to what is merely inferred, or to a conjecture or fiction; a datum of experience, as distinguished from the conclusions that may be based on it."

Notice that this dictionary statement has

two elements in it: 1) what actually is the case; 2) our certainty about what is the case. Lawrence E. Johnson, who agrees with neither Austin nor Strawson, argues that the second element, the emphasis on certainty, is the key to the meaning of fact. He says that it is a mistake to make facts into entities. All that fact-talk adds to the truth of propositions is "the illocutionary force of certifying the adequacy of the evidence for the propositions."[12] That the word 'fact' is used to emphasize certainty one can readily concede. That this usage is the primary role of fact is not so easily conceded. First of all, the actual occurrence of something grounds the certainty, not the other way round, so that what certainty we ever have is derived from the actual occurrence. Second, this emphasis on certainty ignores the origin of the word 'fact.' Dictionaries agree that its origin is the Latin word 'factum' which is the past participle of the verb facere, which means to do. The Latin factum means "that which is done, a deed, act, exploit, achievement."[13] What the Classical as well as the

Scholastic Latin *factum* emphasized was that something has already taken place. A future thing or event is not yet actual and therefore is not a fact. A seed is actual; the plant from this seed is not yet actual. In Aristotelian terms, we can say that the actual is distinguished both from the potential—what is able to be—and from what is becoming—what is in the process of going from the potential to the actual. The central point is that fact is grounded in the actual and it is this known actuality that justifies whatever certainty we possess.[14]

Note well that the core of this meaning of fact is actuality or existence, not just existence in nature. I may, for example, oppose fact to fiction, provided I mean by fiction that which is thought to be in nature when it is not, as in mirrors or false statements. Fiction in this sense means the non-actual. There is, however, another meaning to fiction, i.e. when applied to the characters and events that exist in the imagination of the novelist. Here fiction does not mean the non-actual; it means the actual in the imagination of the artist.

If the central meaning of fact is the actual, I see no reason for not saying that the novelist deals with facts. Certainly he does not deal with facts in nature, nor does he say his facts are in nature, but just as certainly he deals with what is actual in his imagination, and this he captures in his language. Consequently I feel justified in saying that the literary artist deals with facts just as much as any thinker does, though with different sorts of fact. All that is needed to ground a fact is actual existence.[15]

Facts, of course, are more than their ground. Beyond the actual, fact implies a relation to knowledge. Even so-called "unknown facts" are the actual not yet known but knowable; the non-knowable cannot be a fact for us. Both the knowable and what we know are aspects of being. Thus fact has a leg in both the world of knowledge—*aspects* of things are in knowledge—and in the world of things—facts are aspects of *things*. It is this straddling two worlds that accounts for the double usage of fact for statements and for brute facts.

The opposition we noted in this usage disappears when we see why a fact is in the world of things and why it is also in knowledge.

Facts, then, are not things but aspects of things. Any one thing grounds countless facts. This book, for example, is made up of paper and cloth and ink, plus some thread and glue; its pages are uniform in size; it is philosophical; it is the publisher's to reprint; it is yours to resell but not to reprint; and so on. The "and so on" does not mean that the facts this one book presents have been nearly exhausted. It means the opposite, namely, that since no one is likely to finish listing all the facts about this book, there is no point in continuing beyond the spot where it is clear that such a list would never end. Thus facts are not just things. The number of facts is always greater than the number of things. Facts are aspects of things, i.e. the things as present here and now to a knowing power.

This is the reason why one thing yields endless facts. The order is not this: that first one knows the thing and then some fact or aspect of it. The order is the reverse. It is by knowing aspects that one knows the thing. Take a tuning fork and strike it lightly. Its production of sound waves is one aspect of this tuning fork, one presentable only to the sense of hearing. If a man had only one sense, that of hearing and no other sense, he would know only sounding things, and if this fork were not producing sound waves, he would not know it. For hearing, then, to exist is to be sounding and to be sounding is to exist. This aspect of sounding is a fact to hearing; it is not a fact to sight. Thus a fact is an aspect of a thing by which it is presentable to a knowing power.

Every fact presents itself to the human mind as something that has about it more to be known. This "more" stands as an invitation to the mind to discover the mystery the thing contains. It does so by presenting itself as first being itself and then not being other things. If there were only one fact, say one red apple and absolutely nothing else, red apple would cause no wonder to a mind that happened on the scene—*per impossibile,* for then there would be more than the red apple. To exist would be to be apple, to be apple would also be to be red, to exist then would be to be red apple. Everything would fit neatly, with no parts left over. But once there is a second fact, say, a green apple, then the mind would question the facts. First, how does green differ from red? Second, how does green or red differ from apple, seeing that apple in one instance is green and red in the other? Now if the mind wants to clarify this mystery, it will have to discover what color is.

This, of course, is only one invitation these facts would present. Some others are: the chemical constitution of apples, the atomic structure of matter, the genesis of apples as fruit, their role as possible property, their trade value. Beyond such questions there are countless others, including the invitation to discuss how there can be two apples, or how two apples can be one—that is, apple—, or how there can be apples at all, since they were not before they began to be. To explain one of these aspects is not to exclude all mystery from the facts. At most, it makes progress toward understanding part of the mystery contained in the fact of two colored apples.

To see this last point, let us consider Newton's explanation of color.[16] Using experimental facts, he concludes that color is a property of rays of light, that different colors are due to the different kinds (or lengths) of light rays. Then he gives the reason why bodies appear colored, because of the property they have of reflecting some rays more copiously than others. In this way the mystery of colored-appearing bodies has been somewhat reduced to knowledge by giving the cause of such appearance.

I say "somewhat" because there is mystery left in the fact of colored bodies. First, regarding the structure of color. According to Newton, color is determined by the length of light ray. But this raises a problem. The length of a light ray is not the ray; it is only its length. Then if color follows the length of the ray and length is not the ray, then it is not the ray that is colored, only its length is. In other words, color is not the ray of light even though the ray is colored. Very mysterious, indeed, when something both is and is not: the light ray is not color but is nevertheless colored, and color is not the light ray even though light rays are colored. The questions being raised here are not ones that can be solved by experimentation, and for that reason one has no right to expect Newton or any physicist to consider them. My only point is that all the mystery of the fact of color has not been resolved by Newton's explanation.

The same holds for Newton's cause of bodies appearing colored. The reason why they appear colored, he said, is the quality they have of reflecting rays of a certain length more copiously than rays of other lengths. Once he found the cause why bodies appeared colored, he could then substitute part of the facts—reflecting bodies—for another part of the facts— colored rays. Given color, you have bodies reflecting various rays of light; given bodies so reflecting, you have color. The advantage of causal explanation is that once the cause is found, you can substitute it for the effect. Then one can turn attention to the cause and neglect the effect, since it is precontained in its cause. This ideal of explanation is operative in the natural sciences under the rubric of prediction. And this is achieved, if one wants to know what effect will show up when a given light hits a given body. Yet in the order of knowledge, the ideal of identifying cause and effect never fully succeeds. The reason is that one fact in the order of being is not the other; the cause and the effect remain distinct facts. In Newton's explanation the reflecting body is not the ray it reflects, the body is not its reflecting even though it is reflecting rays, and no amount of equating will reduce the stubborn non-identity of cause and effect. Some unity, some explanation has been achieved, some not achieved. That is, mystery is still present even within causal explanation.

I have indicated two roles of fact as mystery. First, fact reveals itself as what needs explanation and thereby encourages men to find the causes of facts, giving rise to the arts and sciences. Secondly, it keeps the mind living by constantly revealing itself anew so that the work of the arts and sciences in principle is never finished. Both roles of fact must be kept in sharp focus. When man forgets this second role of fact as mystery, his desire for more precise knowledge easily blinds him to the real meaning of facts. They lose their proper right to be the inexhaustible ground of the intellectual life and are reduced to mere means used to forge man's arts and sciences. Facts then exist for the sciences, not the sciences for the facts. A strange inversion, yet one congenial to the desire to get rid of mystery by reducing it to science.

IV

One way to meet the problem of mystery is to say that everything is fully explainable in principle even though ~~not~~ not actually explained so far. In other words, there is no such thing as mystery; there is only a temporarily mysterious state of affairs. Two reasons make this solution suspect. First, it is hardly warranted by the facts that at present remain mysterious. Second, it indicates a hope based on past successes achieved precisely by selecting only certain facts. The ones not selected remain outside the science and possibly outside any science.

A second way to evade mystery is to manipulate some facts on principle. Not that any serious thinker just decides out of a clear sky to do violence to the facts. The obvious relationship of knowledge and fact blocks such a move. He can, however, easily manhandle facts in the name of knowledge. Thus Descartes, in the name of clear and distinct ideas, removed all sensible qualities of things and put them in the knowing subject. And Leibniz by his principles of identity and sufficient reason reduced being to its intelligibility. But what is more interesting is that thinkers in the name of some facts exclude other facts. Take the case of Hume, who considered the rationalists—Descartes and Leibniz—to be the source of all philosophical error, because they made things fit their knowledge. Yet in the name of some facts Hume effectively excluded others. His first step was to say what a human mind can know: "All the perceptions of the human mind resolve themselves into two distinct kinds, which I shall call IMPRESSIONS and IDEAS . . . and under this name [impressions] I comprehend all our sensations, passions and emotions, as they make their first appearance in the soul. By *Ideas* I mean the faint images of these in thinking and reason. . . ."[17] The point to notice here is that ideas are not as reliable as the impressions they derive from, while impressions are original and most reliable and must ground all knowledge of fact. The medieval Scholastics had said that there was nothing in the intellect that was not first in the senses. Hume says that there is nothing in the intellect that is not better in the senses. And by this move he effectively excludes some very important aspects of reality, such as substance, self, spirit, consciousness (unless you are willing to call this sentiment), obligation, and the role of reason in morals.[18]

There are other ways of getting rid of some facts by using other facts as the reason. Take the strategy used by Charles L. Stevenson. Using moral language as his starting point, he concludes from a long analysis of ordinary language that "moral judgments are concerned with *recommending* for approval and disapproval."[19] He explains that when one says, "This is good," he is saying, "I approve of this; you approve of it too."[20] There is more here, he says, than just the mere indication of approval; there is also and especially the actual exercise of approving. Consequently, ethical terms are primarily attitude-expressing and for this reason are emotive.[21] In the name of facts uncovered by language analysis, the whole order of moral facts has been reduced to the non-cognitive.

A more radical surgery on facts was developed by the Logical Positivists. A. J. Ayer says: "The assumptions on which

Hume was relying were taken up by the Logical Positivists and embodied in what came to be known as the principle of verification. . . ."[22] Hume's position to which Ayer refers, was expressed forcefully in the last four pages of his *Enquiry Concerning Human Understanding*. Hume had just divided all valid knowing into two types: abstract knowledge concerning quantity and number which is capable of demonstration and thought about matters of fact which is incapable of demonstration. He ends the *Enquiry* with this statement, "When we run over libraries, persuaded of these principles, what havoc must we make? If we take in our hand any volume; of divinity or school metaphysics, for instance; let us ask, '*Does it contain abstract reasoning concerning quantity or number?*' No. '*Does it contain any experimental reasoning concerning matters of fact and existence?*' No. Commit it to the flames; for it can contain nothing but sophistry and illusion."[23] I have quoted this passage from Hume because it suggests what the Logical Positivists did with their theory of the verification principle. This principle can be stated in two ways: first, as the way to determine what an empirical proposition means; second, as the way to determine if such propositions have any cognitive meaning at all. In either case, the principle limits cognitive meaning to what can be verified by observation. Propositions that cannot be so verified or falsified are said to have no cognitive meaning. In this way, also in the name of some facts, all the facts that invited metaphysical or esthetic or moral reasoning are decreed to be meaningless for knowledge.

Again, there is always the temptation that arises from the extraordinary success of the natural sciences. Why should not all knowledge be scientific? Or put in another way: Why should not the natural sciences answer all questions? The position that opts for the omnicompetence of the natural sciences is today known as Naturalism. Though it developed out of Materialism, Naturalism does not hold that all reality consists in matter. Nor does it hold that all phenomena can be spoken of in only one way, the way of science. What it does hold, however, is first that whatever exists can be satisfactorily explained in natural terms, where "natural" means a scientific or causal explanation; and second that where more than one explanation can be given, the scientific explanation takes precedence over any other. As William H. Walsh says of Naturalism, ". . . it is a theory of first principles, and it draws its principles from science."[24] This means, for example, that the actions and decisions of man are not best explained by his reasons for acting; they are best explained by a causal explanation just as chemical and mechanical reactions are. A contemporary example of Naturalism is the movement now called "Sociobiology," which proposes to explain all social behavior by genetic variations.[25]

I have given four examples of ways that men have used to limit relevant facts. These examples have two common characteristics that need pointing out. First of all, each of them is a case of partial scepticism. Only some facts are permitted to yield knowledge; the others that common sense might be inclined to accept are excluded from knowledge. Speaking of minds that cut out some facts, Kurt Vonnegut says that they "might be likened unto a system of gears whose teeth have been filed off at random." The dismaying thing about such minds, he says, "is that any given gear, though mutilated, will have at its circumference unbroken sequences of teeth that are immaculately maintained, that are exquisitely machined. . . . The missing teeth, of course, are simple, obvious truths available and comprehensible even to a ten-year-old, in most cases."[26] Such scepticism, even though partial, is not a likely solution for one with the faith. The man who thinks that the world was made by an intelligent God has no reason to doubt and many reasons to affirm that all of the world is in principle intelligible even if mysterious. And if he also thinks, as St. John says (John 1:1-18), that the world was made according to the Word of God and this Word became truly human, he also has a concrete hope[27] that all truth can be unified in the Person of Christ and consequently that scepticism looks very much like implicit denial of his faith.

The second common characteristic of these examples is that all of them arrive at their partial scepticism from a desire for better knowledge, in the name of which they get rid of recalcitrant facts. That is, their respect for knowledge takes priority over their respect for facts. They begin with their knowledge and through that enter the world of beings. That contemporary philosophers find this approach through knowledge or language congenial only says that they are progeny, willing or unwilling, of the Father of Modern Philosophy, René Descartes, who has also been called the originator of subjectivity.[28] In defense of their position, they can contend that since the intellectual enterprise consists essentially of both thought and things, it makes no difference where one begins, with thought of things or with things thought of. The truth behind this contention is that the two factors, thought and things always come out even, with no remainders. The only things you will ever know are the things you think of, and the things you think of are the only things you will ever know. True as this is, there is more to the issue. The more is this: Which, thought or things, has the last say? Which is the norm, which is the normized? Which is the measure, which the measured? The answer to these questions depends on the entry point. If we enter things through knowledge, then knowledge has the last say; contrariwise, if we enter knowledge through things, then things have the last say. The reason is clear enough: the entry or the beginning point supplies the given, i.e. the first principle, that the other must respect. In other words, what has the first say must also have the last say, for it is the beginning that raises the questions that the answers must fit in order to be answers.

V

Because of the importance of this last question, I propose to give my reasons for saying that things should be our entry to

knowledge and that things should therefore be the norm and measure of our
knowledge. My first reason is taken from
common sense based on the genesis of
knowledge in the individual. We begin
conscious life by discovering things around
us,[29] then the persons around us and finally
we discover, more or less successfully, our-
selves. Only after that do we become curi-
ous about our knowledge. As a Johnny-
come-lately knowledge supposes all of our
contact with things from which it is derived. It seems most unlikely that if in its
early reaches knowledge was fully dependent on things, in its later reaches it would
suddenly become master of the house and
make "what is" depend on our knowledge
of it.

This common sense argument can be bol-
stered by a consideration that A. J. Ayer
develops. He is discussing the view of Sir
Arthur S. Eddington, who presents himself
as sitting down to write at "two tables,"
one of which has extension and "it is com-
paratively permanent, it is coloured, above
all it is *substantial*. . . . My scientific table

is mostly emptiness, sparcely scattered in this emptiness are numerous electric charges rushing about with great speed; but their combined bulk amounts to less than a billionth of the bulk of the table itself."[30] The implication is that the two tables, the one of common experience and the other of science, cannot co-exist. What Ayer notes is that any explanation which says that physical objects cause my perception supposes that I already have perceived the object. "It is only because I can, through perception, independently establish the fact that the table is here in front of me, that I can subsequently explain my seeing in terms of its effect on me."[31] Recall our example of Newton's explanation of color. Does this explanation justify the conclusion that things are not themselves colored. Ayer answers, "What then becomes of the argument that causal conditions of perception make it improbable that we ever perceive things as they really are? The answer is that it too is out of order; it has no standing on the primitive level. Our criteria for reality have in the first instance to be formed in terms of how things appear to us. We have nothing alse to go by."[32] I add only that an explanation which explains one's experience by explaining it away has something suspect about it.

My second argument starts from a checkable fact about speculative knowledge. I see and feel the desk at which I am writing. Before I entered the room I neither saw nor felt it. What happened in this process of knowing? Without going into the mechanics of vision and feeling, I can say that I was changed. I went from not seeing to seeing the desk and from not feeling to feeling it. What happened to the desk? Did it change because sensed by me? The desk is what it was before and after my sensing it. This would seem to ground the position that knowledge about what is changes only the knower. Moreover, it changes him in not just any way, but in such a way that he is now desk-seer and desk-feeler. This point can be stated, as we said above, by saying that the knower becomes qualified or specified in terms of the thing known. And I take this to be a good reason for saying that things should measure or determine knowledge rather than that our knowledge should measure or determine things, i.e. that commitment to facts is the proper stance of knowledge.

VI

This is also the stance of the faith. I indicated earlier that respect for God and his redeeming action translates itself into respect for the things God created and redeemed. I want to emphasize this point here. Christian faith is solidly committed to all facts and the mystery inherent in them. And even though some of these facts are open only to faith, they nevertheless are facts and not theories. Christian revelation can easily be confused with dogmas and doctrines. These are not the ground of Christianity; they are at most statements made by theologians or even Church authorities and expressing in human words what one age or culture thought appropriate to express this Christian revelation.

The expressions may be more or less accurate, more or less complete, more or less adequate to any one time or age or culture. But when Christians want to state the structure of revelation, they appeal directly to the facts of faith. For example, the Apostles Creed, in its earlier Latin form, reads in this way:

1. I believe in God, the Father Almighty
2. And in Christ Jesus, His only-begotten Son, our Lord,
3. Who was born of the Holy Spirit and Virgin Mary,
4. Who was crucified by Pontius Pilate and was buried.
5. The third day He rose again from the dead;
6. He ascended into heaven, sits at the right hand of the Father, whence He is coming to judge the living and the dead,
7. And in the Holy Spirit,
8. The holy Church,
9. The forgiveness of sin and the resurrection of the body. Amen.[33]

Notice that of the nine distinct items of the Apostles' Creed, all except that of Christ coming as judge and the resurrection of the body appeal to facts, aspects of what already is. That these aspects of reality are open only to knowledge through faith does not exclude their being facts for those who have faith. At any rate, the point I am making is that Christian revelation is a revelation of facts about what God has done and is doing for man.

This same point can be seen in the first page of the "Dogmatic Constitution on Divine Revelation" of the Second Vatican Council in 1965. The first words of the document are: "In His goodness and wisdom, God chose to reveal Himself and to make known to us the hidden purposes of His will (cf. Eph. 1:19) by which through Christ, the Word made flesh, man has access to the Father in the Holy Spirit and comes to share in the divine life (cf. Eph. 2:18, 2 Pet. 1:4). Through this revelation, therefore, the invisible God (cf. Col. 1:15; I Tim. 1:17) out of an abundance of His love speaks to men as friends (cf. Ec.

33:11; Jn. 15:14-15) and lives among them (cf. Bar. 3:39), so that He may invite and take them into fellowship with Himself."[34] Thus Faith is a loyal adherence, not to dogmas or doctrines, but to a personal God, the Facts of Facts. God speaks to men out of love and man's loving response is faith.

We are now ready to state our first conclusion. It is this: The essential role of the faith in a Catholic university is to keep mystery vitally alive in Christian intellectual life. By extension, this is also the role of the Catholic university in Academe: to keep mystery alive in the world of intellect. Knowledge lives on facts. And the Christian factual world is shot through with mystery: the mystery of its origin and existence, the mystery of its history as God's world, the mystery of its finality and on-going salvation. It is this awareness of mystery that demands of the Christian openness to all that is just as this openness to all that is sets the further specific roles the faith plays in a Catholic university. We shall now turn to these.

VII

It may help to begin negatively and clear up any lingering doubts generated by an older misapprehension.[35] It is not the role of the faith to ride herd on the arts and sciences and direct them to allowable conclusions. This is not true in fact and, more importantly, not true in principle. What blocks this procedure in principle is the Christian respect for facts. The arts and sciences begin with aspects of reality, find concepts and principles to unify their facts and draw conclusions these principles and facts justify. Anything that comes between a science's facts and conclusions destroys it as a knowledge, for it arrives at conclusions *only* because of its facts and principles. Were the faith to tell a science what to say, there would be no university, only a parody of one, because there could be no valid natural knowledge present in it. Yet there does seem to be one exception to what I said, the case of sacred theology. Theology, however, is no exception to the principle that the only legitimate way to enter a branch of knowledge is through its facts and principles. Sacred theology is the study of God's revealed actions toward men and man's response to God's actions. Since faith supplies the facts and principles that theology uses to arrive at conclusions, sacred theology is built directly on the facts of faith. No other knowledge in the university gets its facts or its principles from the faith. Consequently, no other knowledge can be controlled or directed by the faith, as we just said.

Now we can turn to the specific positive roles of the faith in a Catholic university. Our definition of a university, used at the beginning of this lecture, will get us started. We said that a Catholic university is a community of potential and actual scholars who wish to carry on their teaching and research within the context of their faith. The notion of context, of course, is applicable to many human activities. We can say that the faith is a context for professional life, for family life, even for political life. More generally, we can say that the faith supplies a philosophy of life. What we are now interested in is precisely the faith as a context for the academic life of learning and research. That is, we are seeking the academic roles of the faith in a Catholic university.

The first and most obvious role of the faith is that it grounds and justifies a department of theology and religious studies. The presence of such a department has multiple consequences. For those having faith it means that they enjoy the opportunity of studying their faith at the level of disciplined intellectual competence. Along with growth in their knowledge of the arts and sciences their faith can be more precisely and fully articulated. Consequently, they are not caught in the impossible bind of trying to unify their advancing knowledge in other fields with a static and simplistic knowledge of their faith. Moreover, when the two grow simultaneously, both the faith and the arts and sciences can be at the service of each other. Those who wish to research questions regarding the faith and their religious life have the aid and the encouragement of trained minds to help them do a cred-

itable job, whether their questions arise
from within the faith or from without it.
When faith is put at the service of knowledge, it both supplies an incentive to better knowing—one realizes that Truth is one
of the names of God—and it reminds the
researcher that there are facts of revelation
as well as facts of immediate experience
and overcomes the narrowness of speciali-
zation by expanding the vision to take in
all that is. When good knowledge is put
at the service of faith, the faith becomes
purified of its cultural accretions and can
thereby become more humanly perfect and
therefore more humanly perfective. The
two knowledges, faith and the arts and
sciences, improving together are more
human than either would be alone.

But all of the university community, not
just the Catholics, gain from the presence
of a theology department. All members of
the university can explore the roots of their
own religious traditions and can study, if
they desire, what the major religions hold
and teach. In this way all are encouraged
to consider as important and critical the

role religion has played in the development of both Western and Eastern cultures. Questions, then, about God and about man and the world as related to God are no longer merely personal questions to be discussed in private with one's pastor or spiritual counsellor. Such questions now become also matters with public standing in the academic community. Issues about God are legitimate university subjects, worthy of everyone's continuing attention.

The second role of the faith in a Catholic university is today and always was one difficult to describe. This role comes from the fact that a majority of the students, faculty and staff are themselves Catholic.[36] That the majority are Catholic is neither a rigidly planned situation[37] nor is it merely accidental. The faith is not a condition for being a member of a Catholic university. No one checks to see who is and who is not a believer. At the same time, it is not accidental either in the sense of what just happens by accident or in the sense of being unimportant. Rather it is what one expects in a university that presents itself unequivocally as Catholic to its prospective students and faculty. Since not all members of the university are Catholic, the faith in this role is not a matter of conscious attention or even a context one can appeal to. A better metaphor than context is that of atmosphere. We can say that the faith operates to establish the atmosphere or climate in which learning and teaching takes place. No one need consciously work at creating it. There is no element or activity present that can be isolated and expanded so as to manipulate this atmosphere. It operates by the mere presence of the faith in the majority of the academic community. One atmospheric image to express this fact is that the faith is like a fine mist. No one particle of the mist is of any critical significance. Yet if you stay in the mist long enough, you will certainly get soaked. In our case, you will become sympathetic to a view of the world as filled with mystery because filled with the causality of God. This view of the world is essential to a Catholic university and sympathy with it is expected of all. But sympathy is not faith, nor does it lead to faith, nor does it demand faith. All it demands is that those present like what they see going on around them.[38]

VIII

There is a third role of the faith. It makes possible the hierarchical ordering of the knowledges present in the university. I say that it makes possible this ordering; it does not itself achieve this ordering. Where would it get the right to do this? It is the office of reason to put order in things. If one wishes to order his knowledges, he will have to find the principle of order in knowledge itself. We have indicated above that knowledge, as being about facts, is controlled by its facts. Here then is a norm of ordering knowledges: If the facts one knowledge deals with have more reality than the facts another deals with, the former is more excellent as knowledge. But how are we to decide which facts have more reality? We can turn to common sense, and this would suggest that what continues to be has more reality than what ceases to be. Reason would suggest further that what has existence from itself has more reality than what receives its existence or begins to be from the action of another. And among things that begin to be, those which can cause other things to begin to be have more reality than the things they cause, since the power to cause requires a surplusage in being. Finally, among things that cause, those who individually and freely control their causing actions have more reality than those which have no such control; for example, human beings have more reality than chemicals or trees or animals.

What reason suggests the faith affirms and thus confirms our conclusions concerning where there is more being. We can then confidently apply our principle of order: The more the being, the more excellent is the knowledge that deals with it. For example, Christian theology is the human endeavor of understanding the relation of God and man, first of God's relation to man, then of man's relation to God.

If God has more reality than anything else, as faith holds, then theology, sacred or the natural knowledge of the Absolute, holds high priority in a Catholic university. Next, on the principle that man has more being than purely material things—because, as both faith and reason hold, man can control his own actions and thus can freely relate himself to God—the knowledges that deal with man are more excellent in themselves than knowledges that deal with non-human things. Among the knowledges that deal with man, some more than others enter human reality because they are concerned with human values, the touchstones of creative freedom. Through such free choices man relates himself to God and others and thereby makes himself more or less than what a man can be. That is why these knowledges have been called humanities, because "they consider human values and the experiences of the spirit of man. . . ."[39] The other knowledges of man, anthropology, psychology, political science and sociology could conceivably be humanistic had not their practitioners elected to model their thought on value-free science.[40] Finally there are the knowledges dealing with the non-human world, mathematics and the natural sciences. As for the practical or professional knowledges, if we use the same norm, we should say that those dealing with men are more important than those dealing with non-human reality.

The precise meaning of this ordering of knowledges according to their intrinsic excellence can be sharpened by saying what it does not mean. First, it does not mean that some knowledges are human and some are not. Such a view is nonsense on any level. On that of reason, all achievements that crown man's reasonable endeavors are seen to be fully human. On the level of revelation, this truth is even more obvious. The Catholic who understands the implication of the Incarnation of the Word of God in Christ realizes that the Incarnation sanctifies all reasonable human endeavors and makes them potentially divine. This clearly applies to all knowledges in the university. Second, this ordering of knowledges says nothing about the quality of the instruction and research in various knowleges. Consequently, it does not mean that some subjects are well-taught and well-researched, and others are treated carelessly. Every university with any self-respect will look for high quality in all of its knowledges. Where it cannot, for whatever reason, do a good job, common sense suggests that it ought to cut such knowledges from its offerings. The ordering of knowledges pertains only to those already on board; the ordering done is purely from the relation of a knowledge to the facts that it deals with.[41] Third, this ordering of knowledges does not say which knowledge is the most certain—mathematics is; or which is the more progressive—the sciences are; or which is the most useful—the professions are; or which is the most practical—the one that helps you do what you want to do. All it says is which knowledge is *as knowledge* more excellent.

But having said this it says what is most important to the intellectual life. For the human intellect, by nature made to know what is, also has a further thrust to know

why the facts are as they are. The evidence
for this is the arts and sciences. Moreover,
we can see this thrust in ordinary daily
life, for the human mind is unhappy with
disorder. Suppose you entered this hall
today and found all the seats piled high
in the center of the room. Your mental re-
action would be, "What a mess!" You en-
quire about this situation and you are told,
"The chairs are piled up because we want
to burn them." Immediately the mind is
no longer offended by the apparent disorder. Indeed, the pile of chairs is no
longer a mess but something that makes
sense. The sense is based on the unity
among the facts. In practical knowledge
unity comes from the end, i.e. we want to
burn the chairs. In speculative knowledge
the unity comes from the concepts and
principles first discovered in the facts and
then used to put order among them. Newton, for example, put order into the experimental facts of classical mechanics by
means of the four concepts: mass, momen-
tum, inertia, and force. Using these concepts he could understand, i.e. find unity

in, the facts of mechanics. What is true of one situation—the piled chairs—and what is true of one experimental science—Newtonian mechanics—is also true of the total contents of the mind. To hold one's knowledge of the arts and sciences as so many disparate and suspicious tenants under one roof, like animals in a zoo, is no ideal for one's intellectual life. What is needed is understanding, i.e. unity, among all our knowledges. Here we see the full meaning of the role of the faith as ordering knowledges; it makes possible a unity of order among all the knowledges, and this makes possible a unified intellectual life. The older term for this was Christian wisdom.

IX

The fourth and final role of the faith in a Catholic university is that it supplies the values the university advocates and fosters. Commonly, this is given as the main role of the faith when administrators address this issue. They say that the distinctiveness of the Catholic university is that it advocates Christian values. By this they could refer to official statements about the goals and general policies of the school that explicitly refer to Christian values. They could also refer to the program offered and the requirements in course work for each program. Or they could refer to administrative directives in the execution of programs, say, the Christian emphasis on the infinite value of the individual. Again, they could refer to the advocacy of research programs that look to issues important to Christians. Finally, they could appeal to the presence of a campus ministry. All of these are clearly ways in which a university can advocate Christian values.

Important as all of these administrative acts are, all of them look to and depend on something other than themselves. What I mean can be seen if we consider the campus ministry. This activity is conceived as a practicum where those students who wish can learn in action ways to live out Christian values. The soul of this activity is the insights achieved in theological learning. Without such knowledge a campus ministry would not be an integral part of a university. And something very similar holds true of all administrative acts. The soul of all university operations must be the knowledge developed and taught in the university. It would seem then that we have not gotten down to the real advocacy of Christian values until we see how teaching and research stand relative to such values.

Here we run into a serious problem. Can you teach values? You can, of course, sponsor values by negative and positive reinforcement, by counselling and advice, by exhortation and preaching. None of these is teaching. There is only one way for teaching to touch values: If values are grounded in being and being can be taught, then teaching could indirectly get at values through being. However, this could never be achieved if values are subjective—dependent on the one who evaluates. The common opinion today is that indeed values are subjective. One contemporary way to say this is to speak of "creating our own values." It is easy to see that people have different preferences and choices, and it is likewise easy to conclude that they do in fact evaluate things differently. Some value a university education; some could not care less about it. Then it is very easy to conclude that values are subjective and depend on the persons making the evaluation.

Against this position, I will begin by saying that the above view of preference and choice confuses value and motive. These two should be distinguished, because, as I contend, value is mainly objective and motive is mainly subjective. Note the factors in value: 1) that which has value, and 2) the subject to which it appears valuable. By "mainly objective" I want to contend that the more critical of the two factors in value is the first, the thing that has value. Let us look at some facts. Suppose you are thinking of choosing a college education. You consider what is good about it. By good, I mean what profit will it bring to you or to others. Since this profit comes from acquiring the education, you must consistently think that the education can confer this profit. This profit-conferring quality of the college education is its value or good. Either this value belongs to the education or our choosing *it* for the profit *it* confers is radically unintelligible. Why choose it rather than something else? The only reason is that you think that the education can confer profit on you that nothing else can. Since choosing a college education is not unintelligible, the conclusion must be that value or profit-conferring is a quality of the college education, i.e. of the object chosen. Even when we find that we are mistaken and the profit sought does not eventuate from getting what we chose, we do not conclude that value is subjective. We conclude that we were mistaken in thinking (or hoping) that the object could confer this profit on us. No such conclusion would be possible if value were mainly subjective. Were it the case that our valuing a thing determined its value, our very desiring it would give it the value desired, and we could never be mistaken as long as we chose consciously. This is against the facts. Consequently we conclude in cases of such misjudgment that the object did not have the value we thought it had. That is, we conclude, or should conclude, that values are mainly objective, because value originates in the object.

We can say now that value is what is known as good or profit-conferring and therefore the possible object of desire and choice. What I consider good I can also desire. Value is the choosability of a thing or an action. But choosability is not yet choice. Here motive enters the picture. When the choosability of a thing moves me to actual choice of it, we have a motive, i.e. what moved me to make a choice. Motive is needed to get the choosable into the state of being actually chosen. This motive is needed because what is choosable from one viewpoint may not be choosable from another. For example, a favorite desert for one on a diet is both choosable by reason of taste and not choosable by reason of health. If the dieter eats the pie, then we would say that he made the taste a motive for his action; it moved him to choose the pie, while the good of health, still a value in itself, is not now a motive, for it does

not now move him to choose it. Motives
are personal and private, the point on
which freedom rides. But values are
aspects of things as choosable. Whether or
not I make a value my present motive
does not either make or unmake the
choosability of things. All I can do is decide which value will be a motive for my
choice here and now.

Looked at this way, values are the aspects of things as choosable. In order to be
choosable, knowledge is required as a condition. Then value is the known desirability of a thing or an action. Here we are
down to the two basic conditions for things
having value: knowledge and desirability.
Of these two, knowledge comes first in
time, for it specifies the subject in terms of
the things and this gives an object. Then
comes desirability, which arises from the
already-known object as having value. This
dependence of desirability on knowledge
also shows its ultimate ground in being.
That is why nothing is not and cannot be
the object of desire; only what is or can be
or can be thought to be able to be is de-

sirable. Here, then, is the metaphysical reason for saying that value is mainly objective: Desirability depends on knowledge and knowledge depends on being, so that the ultimate ground of desirability is being.[42] This is also the reason for saying that in principle the more the being, the more desirability or value it grounds.

Given this intimate connection between knowledge and values, if we can successfully decide which knowledge is the more excellent because it deals with what possesses more reality, we can also put a reasonable order among values. The faith makes possible a firm decision about what has more reality. It also, therefore, makes possible a firm decision about what is more valuable. This approach to values through knowledge is, I submit, the proper way for values to come into university education; the knowledges say what has more being; the known being is the ground for values and is then open to become motives of choice. Any other approach to values is destructive of learning and research. To emphasize motives in the classroom is to interfere with human freedom. To emphasize values directly leaves them grounded only in sentiment and good will. But to emphasize what is, all that is, is to proceed from what is fundamental to both knowledge and valuation—and even hopefully to justifiable motivation.[43]

X

By way of concluding this lecture, I could simply summarize the general role of the faith in a Catholic university—its insistence on mystery and all that is—and then its four specific roles: 1) as grounding a theology department; 2) as being present in the majority of the university members; 3) as making possible a hierachy of knowledges that gives unity to the intellectual life; and 4) at the same time making possible a reasonable order among values. I prefer, however, to show in a concrete example rather than in abstract categories how the faith aids understanding. I shall take the case of understanding the goal of undergraduate education.

The American university has developed

under the influence of the liberal tradition, which proposed the ideal of man as "the master of all situations and bound to none." This ideal puts emphasis on personal development in order to arrive at being a self-sufficient person, one who has the fewest possible limitations and therefore the greatest freedom. It is the educated person who is prepared for life, who can use personal powers to the full, who can see and seize opportunities for self-expression and thereby attain self-fulfillment. In short, it is the educated person who can be free. Psychologically this idea can be referred to as maturity or "self-realization," which is considered the single ultimate human value.[44] On this view, education is self-development that leads to self-expression that leads to self-fulfillment or maturity.

As good as this view of the goal of undergraduate education is—and who in his right mind can deny that education is perfective of the student?—it is incomplete in the eyes of a Catholic. There are two ways to see this incompleteness. The first looks to the emphasis on self, which a Christian finds excessive. The Christian understands knowledge as man's way of entering the world of things and persons; his understanding of love is man's concern for the other, not for self. As selves we are individuals, separated from one another, divided from all else and therefore fundamentally lonely and small. By going out of self through knowledge and love we enter the expansive world and can thereby share in all of God's grand creation. Rather than self being central to our education or our lives—self-development, self-expression, self-fulfillment—what is central is that we know what is most real—God—and consequently are obliged to be like God in our concern for the good of others. Christ put this truth graphically: "Any one who loves his life loses it; and anyone who hates his life in this world will keep it in eternal life" (John 12:25). That is, you gain life in this world and the next not by concern for self or by clinging to self, but by letting go of self and thereby gaining the world of what is.

A second way to see this same point is

to look to the notion of maturity. Since maturity is the psychological term used today for human perfection, we are all supposed to strive for a mature personality. This maturity is generally represented as the complete all-round development of human powers and results in a balanced life, a wholeness that is marked by personal control, calm stability, and competence in meeting the problems of life. No doubt a Christian should be mature, but for him maturity goes beyond a balanced competence. It consists rather in knowledge of what most is and in relating one's thought and action to what is the most reality, i.e. to God. We shall call this, with Marjorie Reeves, "singleness of purpose."[45] This position follows directly from what we said of knowledge being about what is. If God is the most reality and we grow in humanness by knowing and ordering our lives to what most is, then full Christian maturity consists in the singleness of purpose by which we relate our lives to God. This was the wholeness of Christ: he came to do the will of his Father and that is what he did every moment of life from his birth to his resurrection. When he was asked how men should approach God, i.e. pray, he gave them the prayer which says: "Thy will be done on earth as in heaven" (Mt. 6:10-11). Christ was one with his Father because he did the will of his Father. We Christians become whole or mature in the same way, by becoming one with the Father. This is the single purpose of Christian life and is for that reason also the single final purpose of Christian education; and it is so precisely to the extent that education is preparation for life and Christian education is preparation for Christian life.

NOTES

1. Ladislas Orsy, S.J., "Interaction Between University and Church," *The Catholic Mind* LXXIII, no. 1290, February 1975, pp. 38-57. Orsy contends that the Church has a duty to be university-minded. Concerning the question: How can the Church be university-minded?, he says: "Yet for the future of the Church this may be a most important question of this century, because to be university-minded means to insert the gospel into our cultural mileu and to use reflective, critical and scholarly intelligence to communicate rightly the content of our faith. In these matters, the Church does not have an option. It has a need and a duty" (p. 50).

2. That the American Catholic universities so conceive themselves is clear in the "Land O'Lakes Statement" made under the auspices of the North American Region of the International Federation of Colleges and Universities, July 23, 1967. The authors of the Statement were 26 of the most important Catholic educators in the U.S., Canada, and Latin America. See *America* 117, no. 1, August 12, 1967. See also Neil G. McCloskey, S.J. (ed.), *The Catholic University: A Modern Appraisal*, Notre Dame: University of Notre Dame Press, 1970. The "Land O'Lakes Statement" is reprinted as an appendix to this volume.

3. *Being and Having*, trans. Katharine Farrer, Glasgow: The University Press, 1949. He says: "A problem is something which I meet, which I find complete before me, but which I can therefore laý siege to and reduce. But a mystery is something in which I myself am involved, and it can

therefore only be thought of as a *sphere where distinction between what is in me and what is before me loses its meaning and its initial validity*" (p. 117; italics his).

4. *The Mystery of Existence*, New York: Appleton-Century-Crofts, 1965, p. 27.

5. Cf. Avery Dulles, S.J., "Mystery (in Theology)," *The New Catholic Encyclopedia* X, New York: McGraw-Hill, 1967, pp. 151-53. Dulles adds a third type of mystery, one supernatural in its factual origin but in principle naturally knowable.

6. By "commitment" I do not mean either an act of faith or an act of love. I mean the act by which I take sides on what is because I see that reality has taken sides before me.

7. Aristotle, *Metaphysics* II, 1, 993b 20; *Ethics* VI, 2, 1139a 26-31.

8. Cf. Gerard Smith. S.J. *Natural Theology*, New York: The Macmillan Company, 1951, pp. 4-6.

9. "Unfair to Facts," in *Philosophical Papers*, Oxford: Clarendon Press, 1961, p. 117.

10. "Truth," *Analysis* 9, no. 6, June 1959. Strawson and Austin argued the question in the "Symposium on Truth," *Aristotelian Society:* Supplement XXIV, 1950, pp. 109-156.

11. Austin, *op. cit.*, p. 111.

12. "A Matter of Fact," *The Review of Metaphysics* XXX, no. 3, March 1977, p. 514. Johnson develops a position introduced by F. A. Tillman, "Facts, Events, and True Statements," *Theoria* XXXII, 1966, Part 2. Tillman's position is: "Fact is an authority-giving device applicable to assertions "(p. 129).

13. C. T. Lewis and C. Short, *A Latin Dictionary*, 1879.

14. Austin states this point in this way: "It seems to me, on the contrary, that to say that something *is* a fact is at least in part precisely to say that it is something in the world: much more than—though perhaps also to a minor extent also—to classify it as being some special kind of something-in-the-world" (*op. cit.*, p. 106; emphasis his).

15. Actual existence is found in three areas: in nature as a subject of existing, in knowledge as an object existing, in love as the beloved existing in the act of love. For the latter type of being, a "desirous way of being," see G. Smith, S.J. and L. Kendzierski, *The Philosophy of Being*, New York: The Macmillan Company, 1961, pp. 103-149.

16. *Opticks*, Book I, Prop. X (New York: Dover, 1952) p. 179: "These Colours arise from hence, that some natural Bodies reflect some sorts of Rays, others other sorts more copiously than the rest. Minium reflects the least refrangible or red-making Rays most copiously, and thence appears red. Violets reflect the most refrangible most copiously, and thence have their Colours, and so on of other Bodies. Every Body reflects the Rays of its own Colour more copiously than the rest, and from their excess and predominance in the reflected Light has its Colour."

17. *A Treatise on Human Nature*, Book I, Part I, Sect. I, ed. T. H. Green and T. H. Grose, 2 vols., London: Longmans, Green and Co., 1909, Vol. 1, p. 311; emphasis his.

18. Roberto Unger argues (in *Knowledge and Politics*, New York: The Free Press, 1975, pp. 42-62)

that Hume supplies the psychological foundation for classical liberalism by his notion of the relation of intellect to will. Hume says: "Reason is, and ought to be a slave of passions, and can never pretend to any other office than to serve and obey them" (*op. cit.*, Book IV, Part II, Sect. III, Vol. 2, p. 195). A morality of sentiment logically gives preference to sentiments and these are best served by freedom.

19. *Ethics and Language*, New Haven: Yale University Press, 1944, p. 13; emphasis his.

20. *Ibid.*, p. 22. His wording is, "I approve of this; do so as well."

21. *Facts and Values*, New Haven: Yale University Press, 1973, p. 65.

22. *The Central Questions of Philosophy*, New York: Holt, Rinehart and Winston, 1973, p. 23.

23. *Enquiry Concerning Human Understanding and Concerning the Principles of Morals*, ed. L. A. Selby-Bigge, 3rd edit., revised by F. H. Nidditch, Oxford: Clarendon Press, 1975, p. 168; emphasis his.

24. *Encyclopaedia Britannica*, 15th ed., 1043-47, Vol. 12, Macropaedia, "Metaphysics," p. 26.

25. See *Time*, Vol. 109, no. 16, April 18, 1977, pp. 54-63.

26. *Mother Night*, New York: Harper and Row, 1961, pp. 168-169.

27. See William J. Richardson, S.J., "Pay Any Price? Break Any Mold?," *America* 116, no. 17, April 29, 1967, p. 626.

28. See Hiram Caton, *The Origin of Subjectivity: An Essay on Descartes*, New Haven: Yale University Press, 1973.

29. Max Scheler (*Man's Place in Nature*, trans. Hans Meyerhoff, New York: The Noonday Press, 1961) argues that even plant life exhibits its relating to what is outside it. "The vital feeling of the plant is oriented toward its medium, toward the growing into this medium in accordance with direction like 'above' and 'below' . . ." (p. 9). Note that this position gives some standing to the much derided argument of *solvitur ambulando*, i.e. solving a problem by action rather than argument.

30. *The Nature of the Physical World*, New York: The Macmillan Company, 1928, pp. ix-x.

31. *The Central Questions of Philosophy*, New York: Holt, Rinehart, Winston, 1973, p. 87.

32. *Ibid.*, p. 88.

33. Henry Denzinger, *Enchiridion Symbolorum*, 30th ed., trans. R. T. DeFerrari, St. Louis: Herder Book Co., 1957, pp. 4-5.

34. Walter M. Abbott, S.J., ed., *Documents of Vatican II*, New York: Guild Press, 1966, p. 112.

35. I refer to the kind of statement frequently attributed to George Bernard Shaw to the effect that a Catholic university is a contradiction in terms.

36. I have no national figures to show that in a Catholic university the majority is Catholic. I have reason to believe that no national figures on this point have ever been collected. At Marquette University there are figures on the percentage of Catholic students, but none on the faculty or staff. Here are the student figures for the last four years: in 1976, 79.4; in 1975, 79.9; in 1974, 80.1; and in 1973, 79.4. A 1974-75 study of fourteen Methodist-relation colleges showed that 31

percent of the 20,000 students were Methodists. See *A College-Related Church: United Methodist Perspectives*, Nashville: National Commission On United Methodist Higher Eduaction, 1976, p. 17.

37. Though none that I know of do, there is no reason in principle why a university could not require that its members be Catholic. Against this. position one can bring the superficially persuasive argument that pluralism is a good thing in any intellectual community. The trouble with this argument is that in principle pluralism could swamp the Catholic atmosphere and thereby negate the justification of the presence of a Catholic university in Academe.

38. All universities in fact set up an atmosphere of one sort or another. People with like training and similar ideals accept and teach patterns of thought that are taken for granted. The fact that a university knows and announces the atmosphere that it lives in is besides a matter of honesty also a protection against masked indoctrination.

39. Otto A. Bird, *Encyclopaedia Britannica*, 15th ed., 1943-47, Macropaedia, Vol. 8, p. 1179.

40. Peter L. Berger says that, owing to his professionally sociological and therefore "value-free" stance, his book (*The Sacred Canopy*, Garden City: Doubleday, 1967) could be read as a treatise on atheism, at least in parts. "The analysis of the contemporary situation with which it ended could easily be read (and, as far as my intentions were concerned, misread) as a counsel of despair for religion in the modern world. For better or for worse, my self-understanding is

not exhausted by the fact that I am a sociologist. I also consider myself a Christian . . ." (*A Rumor of Angels*, Garden City: Doubleday Anchor Books, 1970, p. ix).

41. By this I do not mean that reasons from faith may not be used together with other reasons to exclude some knowledges from a university. Lack of competent personnel, lack of interested students, or lack of finances, any one or any combination of these may force a Catholic university to look to its priorities. It will then appeal to the ordering of knowledges made possible by the faith's acceptance of mystery. But this situation is not derived from the faith; it derives from the presence of some lack. From itself and in principle the faith can accept any knowledge perfective of man who is made for God and give it a place in an hierarchical ordering.

42. For a full explanation of the desirable—being as good—see G. Smith, S.J., and L. Kendzierski, *The Philosophy of Being*, New York: The Macmillan Company, 1961, pp. 103-146.

43. How such knowledge does in fact relate to motivation is considered in my *Teaching and Morality* (Chicago: Loyola University Press, 1968), Chapter 6, "Reasoned Assents and Moral Choice," pp. 186-213.

44. For a statement of this ideal see Abraham Maslow, "Psychological Data and Value Theory," in A. Maslow (ed.), *New Knowledge in Human Values*, New York: Harper and Row, 1959. Maslow does not emphasize self in opposition to others, but even love of the other is presented as fulfilling a *need* of the individual. "Also not to be overlooked is the fact that these love needs

involve both giving *and* receiving love" (*Motivation and Personality*, 2nd rev. ed., New York: Harper and Row, 1970 p. 45; emphasis his.) Charlotte Buhler ("Human Life Goals in the Humanist Perspective," *Journal of Humanistic Psychology* VII, no. 1, Spring 1967, p. 48) prefers fulfillment to self-realization.

45. *Three Questions in Higher Education*, New Haven: The Hazen Foundation, 1955, p. 28.

The Aquinas Lectures

Published by the Marquette University Press
Milwaukee, Wisconsin 53233

St. Thomas and the Life of Learning (1937) by John F. McCormick, S.J., (1874-1943) professor of philosophy, Loyola University.
SBN 87462-101-1

St. Thomas and the Gentiles (1938) by Mortimer J. Adler, Ph.D., director of the Institute of Philosophical Research, San Francisco, Calif.
SBN 87462-102-X

St. Thomas and the Greeks (1939) by Anton C. Pegis, Ph.D., professor of philosophy, Pontifical Institute of Mediaeval Studies, Toronto.
SBN 87462-103-8

The Nature and Functions of Authority (1940) by Yves Simon, Ph.D., (1903-1961) professor of philosophy of social thought, University of Chicago.
SBN 87462-104-6

St. Thomas and Analogy (1941) by Gerald B. Phelan, Ph.D., (1892-1965) professor of philosophy, St. Michael's College, Toronto.
SBN 87462-105-4

St. Thomas and the Problem of Evil (1942) by Jacques Maritain, Ph.D., professor *emeritus* of philosophy, Princeton University.
SBN 87462-106-2

Humanism and Theology (1943) by Werner Jaeger, Ph.D., Litt.D., (1888-1961) University professor, Harvard University. SBN 87462-107-0

The Nature and Origins of Scientism (1944) by John Wellmuth. SBN 87462-108-9

Cicero in the Courtroom of St. Thomas Aquinas (1945) by E. K. Rand, Ph.D., Litt.D., LL.D., (1871-1945) Pope professor of Latin, *emeritus*, Harvard University. SBN 87462-109-7

St. Thomas and Epistemology (1946) by Louis-Marie Regis, O.P., Th.L., Ph.D., director of the Albert the Great Institute of Mediaeval Studies, University of Montreal.
SBN 87462-110-0

St. Thomas and the Greek Moralists (1947, Spring) by Vernon J. Bourke, Ph.D., professor of philosophy, St. Louis University, St. Louis, Missouri. SBN 87462-111-9

History of Philosophy and Philosophical Education (1947, Fall) by Etienne Gilson of the *Académie française*, director of studies and professor of the history of Mediaeval philosophy, Pontifical Institute of Mediaeval Studies, Toronto. SBN 87462-112-7

The Natural Desire for God (1948) by William R. O'Connor, S.T.L., Ph.D., former professor of dogmatic theology, St. Joseph's Seminary, Dunwoodie, N.Y. SBN 87462-113-5

St. Thomas and the World State (1949) by Robert M. Hutchins, former Chancellor of the University of Chicago, president of the Fund for the Republic. 　　　 SBN 87462-114-3

Method in Metaphysics (1950) by Robert J. Henle, S.J., Ph.D., academic vice-president, St. Louis University, St. Louis, Missouri.
　　　 SBN 87462-115-1

Wisdom and Love in St. Thomas Aquinas (1951) by Étienne Gilson of the *Académie française,* director of studies and professor of the history of Mediaeval philosophy, Pontifical Institute of Mediaeval Studies, Toronto.
　　　 SBN 87462-116-X

The Good in Existential Metaphysics (1952) by Elizabeth G. Salmon, Ph.D., professor of philosophy in the graduate school, Fordham University. 　　　 SBN 87462-117-8

St. Thomas and the Object of Geometry (1953) by Vincent Edward Smith, Ph.D., director, Philosophy of Science Institute, St. John's University. 　　　 SBN 87462-118-6

Realism and Nominalism Revisited (1954) by Henry Veatch, Ph.D., professor and chairman of the department of philosophy, Northwestern University. 　　　 SBN 87462-119-4

Imprudence in St. Thomas Aquinas (1955) by Charles J. O'Neil, Ph.D., professor of philosophy, Villanova University. 　　　 SBN 87462-120-8

The Truth That Frees (1956) by Gerard Smith, S.J., Ph.D., professor of philosophy, Marquette University. SBN 87462-121-6

St. Thomas and the Future of Metaphysics (1957) by Joseph Owens, C.Ss.R., Ph.D., professor of philosophy, Pontifical Institute of Mediaeval Studies, Toronto. SBN 87462-122-4

Thomas and the Physics of 1958: A Confrontation (1958) by Henry Margenau, Ph.D., Eugene Higgins professor of physics and natural philosophy, Yale University.
SBN 87462-123-2

Metaphysics and Ideology (1959) by Wm. Oliver Martin, Ph.D., professor of philosophy, University of Rhode Island. SBN 87462-124-0

Language, Truth and Poetry (1960) by Victor M. Hamm, Ph.D., professor of English, Marquette University. SBN 87462-125-9

Metaphysics and Historicity (1961) by Emil L. Fackenheim, Ph.D., professor of philosophy, University of Toronto. SBN 87462-126-7

The Lure of Wisdom (1962) by James D. Collins, Ph.D., professor of philosophy, St. Louis University. SBN 87462-127-5

Religion and Art (1963) by Paul Weiss, Ph.D. Sterling professor of philosophy, Yale University. SBN 87462-128-3

St. Thomas and Philosophy (1964) by Anton C. Pegis, Ph.D., professor of philosophy, Pontifical Institute of Mediaeval Studies, Toronto.
SBN 87462-129-1

The University In Process (1965) by John O. Riedl, Ph.D., dean of faculty, Queensboro Community College.
SBN 87462-130-5

The Pragmatic Meaning of God (1966) by Robert O. Johann, associate professor of philosophy, Fordham University.
SBN 87462-131-3

Religion and Empiricism (1967) by John E. Smith, Ph.D., professor of philosophy, Yale University.
SBN 87462-132-1

The Subject (1968) by Bernard Lonergan, S.J., S.T.D., professor of Dogmatic Theory, Regis College, Ontario and Gregorian University, Rome.
SBN 87462-133-X

Beyond Trinity (1969) by Bernard J. Cooke, S.T.D.
SBN 87462-134-8

Ideas and Concepts (1970) by Julius R. Weinberg, Ph.D., (1908-1971) Vilas Professor of Philosophy, University of Wisconsin.
SBN 87462-135-6

Reason and Faith Revisited (1971) by Francis H. Parker, Ph.D., head of the philosophy department, Purdue University, Lafayette, Indiana.
SBN 87462-136-4

Psyche and Cerebrum (1972) by John N. Findlay, M.A. Oxon., Ph.D., Clark Professor of Moral Philosophy and Metaphysics, Yale University.
ISBN 0-87462-137-2

The Problem of the Criterion (1973) by Roderick M. Chisholm, Ph.D., Andrew W. Mellon Professor in the Humanities, Brown University.
ISBN 0-87462-138-0

Man as Infinite Spirit (1974) by James H. Robb, Ph.D., professor of philosophy, Marquette University.
ISBN 0-87462-139-9

The Beginning and the Beyond (1975) by Eric Voegelin, Ph.D. In preparation.

Aquinas to Whitehead: Seven Centuries of Metaphysics of Religion (1976) by Charles E. Hartshorne, Ph.D., professor of philosophy, the University of Texas at Austin.
ISBN 0-87462-141-0

The Problem of Evil (1977) by Errol E. Harris, D.Litt., Distinguished Visiting Professor of Philosophy, Marquette University.
ISBN 0-87462-142-8

The Catholic University and the Faith (1978) by Francis C. Wade, S.J., professor of philosophy, Marquette University
ISBN 0-87462-143-7

Uniform format, cover and binding.

Copies of this lecture and the others in the series
are obtainable from:

Marquette University Press
Marquette University
Milwaukee, Wisconsin 53233 U.S.A.